IMAGES OF ENGLAND

SCUNTHORPE

Scunthorpe, *c.* 1893. The flour mill, the school, the Tin Tabernacle, the vicarage and the Primitive Methodist chapel are all visible in this photograph taken from the Chimney of Frodingham Ironworks.

IMAGES OF ENGLAND

SCUNTHORPE

REG & KATHLEEN COOKE

The Blue Bell Flyer. This horse-drawn bus was owned by R.I. Swaby, landlord of the Blue Bell. The driver is thought to be William Parrott who came from the Angel Hotel at Brigg, in the early 1920s to drive it.

We dedicate this book to our children and grandchildren,
Christine, Susan, Peter, Katey and Emily.
Entwined within the pages are their roots.

First published in 1997 by Tempus Publishing
Reprinted 2002

Reprinted in 2008 by
The History Press
The Mill, Brimscombe Port,
Stroud, Gloucestershire, GL5 2QG
www.thehistorypress.co.uk

Reprinted 2013

British Library Cataloguing in Publication Data.
A catalogue record for this book is available from the British Library.

ISBN 978 0 7524 0764 7

Typesetting and origination by
Tempus Publishing Limited.
Printed and bound in England.

Contents

William Dixon, blast-furnace keeper at Trent Ironworks. The only safety clothing that he is wearing are the mole skin trousers as he stands by the open pig iron bed prior to 'tapping' the furnace.

Introduction

The chance re-discovery of ironstone by a shooting party on Brumby Warren in 1858/59 was the catalyst that triggered off the development of ironstone mining, followed quickly by ironmaking and later by steelmaking. This, in turn, resulted in a sudden and continuous influx of people into the area to find work in the new industry.

Prior to this event, the Scunthorpe we know was just five sleepy little villages set in five narrow strips of land. They were Crosby, Scunthorpe, Frodingham, Brumby and Ashby. The oldest of the villages is probably Frodingham, although at the time that the Domesday Book was compiled in 1086 it had been so decimated by Viking raids that there was not enough of the settlement left to warrant its inclusion.

Incidentally, the Scunthorpe area resisted Duke William and it was not until he had put all of the area up to York 'to fire and sword' that he became free to tackle the Domesday Book.

The area was part of Danelaw before 1066 and the names of the villages derive mainly from Scandinavian influence and the probable derivations are old Scandinavian, old English and Anglo-Saxon.

Crosby, (Cropesbi): Krokr, an old Scandinavian word meaning 'in the nook' or a man's name; 'by' is old Scandinavian and means 'farmstead' or 'settlement'. The farmstead in the nook or the settlement of Krokr.

Scunthorpe, (Escumetorp). An old Scandinavian word meaning Skuma, a man's name and 'thorpe', old Scandinavian for outlying settlement. It is probable that Scunthorpe was the outlying settlement, or farmstead, of Skuma, outlying the main settlement of Frodingham.

Frodingham, derives from both Anglo-Saxon and old English. Frod(a) or Fortha is a man's name in old English, 'ingas' is Anglo-Saxon for 'people of' or 'dwellers at', and 'ham' is old English for homestead. The homestead of the people of Fortha.

Brumby, (Brunebi). Bruni is an old Scandinavian man's name or 'brunnr' which means a spring. The farmstead of Bruni or the settlement by the spring.

Ashby, (Aschebi). Aski is old Scandinavian for a man's name or 'askr' which is old Scandinavian for ash tree, but there was a landowner in pre-Norman times called Aschil. He had three sons called Brand, Syric and Sivorth, and it is most likely that Ashby is named after him. The settlement of Aschil.

In 1859, the total population of the five villages was a little over 1,000 people, then the job seekers and their families mushroomed the population. In 1921 the population was around

28,000 and over 70,000 by the 1980s. The building of properties linked the villages together materially but not administratively, there was a lot of rivalry and in some cases, animosity, between the various local boards.

Prior to 1890, the local affairs were controlled by the Sanitary Committee which was responsible to Brigg Rural Council. On 17 October 1890, Scunthorpe became an Urban Authority. In 1894 Brumby and Frodingham parishes joined and were given urban status. In 1897 the idea of a common water supply was rejected because Scunthorpe insisted on having more members on the board. In 1899 Scunthorpe obtained the gas rights to the town.

Scunthorpe made the first application for amalgamation with Frodingham. Frodingham unanimously rejected it and formed an anti-amalgamation committee. In 1904 Dr Berhendt, who was the medical officer for both councils, was sacked by Frodingham because he could have a conflict of interests.

In 1913 Scunthorpe, Crosby and Ashby amalgamated as an Urban District. This left Frodingham and Brumby sandwiched and in 1914 there was the first agreement to look favourably on joining with the new authority but, when Scunthorpe agreed, Frodingham reverted to their previous position and the decision to amalgamate was postponed for the duration of the war. March 1919 saw, at last, the amalgamation of the two authorities. This did not stop ill feeling between members of the new authority and they disagreed about the choice of a name for the new town; should it be Scunthorpe or Frodingham?

It was agreed to call the town Frodingham & Scunthorpe, and later, when the current railway station was built just over the Frodingham boundary in Scunthorpe, London North Eastern Railway (LNER) named the station Scunthorpe & Frodingham and the name stuck. Finally, when borough status was awarded by King Edward VIII, who was never crowned, the word Frodingham was dropped and the town became Scunthorpe.

As the town grew larger the churches and chapels became too small for the increasing congregations and had to rebuild. Other denominations moved into town. This trend was followed by businesses and businessmen and so the town grew and changed. It continues to do so, but now at a slower pace.

We hope that the photographs in this volume give you an image of the past, revive some memories, and preserve the pride we should have, and surely do have, in our beautiful garden town and its founders.

We have tried to select photographs for inclusion that have not been published or, at least, have had very little exposure. Also, we have included a brief chronicle of dates for the duration 1858 to 1950 which is the approximate period covered by the photographs. We hope that this volume finds a place on your coffee table, brings back memories and creates interest to all those who pick it up.

One

Mining and the
Iron and Steel Industry

Casting a blast-furnace at Appleby-Frodingham's South Iron Works in 1956.

Old Ironstone Miners, *c.* 1860. This is believed to be on the site of the first mine somewhere near the Old Courthouse.

Yarborough Pit in the early 1900s. The Ironstone 'Chuckers' at the ore bed and a 'sander' on the trestle/plank walkway can be seen removing the overburden. Walking the planks was a very dangerous job.

Yarborough Mine in the 1930s. This is the Lubecker excavator/dredger used to remove overburden and installed in 1925. The buckets could work in an upward or downward position.

Yarborough Mine in the 1950s. On the skyline the South Iron Works, Redbourn and North Iron Works can be seen.

Trent Iron Works viewed from St John's Church Tower, looking down Dawes Lane. Note the haymaking in the foreground.

View down Dawes Lane in the 1960s. A comparison view with the previous photograph. Redbourn Works and a gas holder can be seen in the distance.

Trent Iron Works. These were Scunthorpe's first ironworks. The first furnace was 'blown-in' on 26 March 1864.

Blowing-up Trent Iron Works in 1935.

Frodingham Iron Works, c. 1896. This was the second works to be built in the town, in 1865. The first and second railway stations can be seen in front of the furnaces and on the far right. Rowland Winn's school for girls and infants, built in 1885, is shown bottom left as also is the builders yard for St John's church.

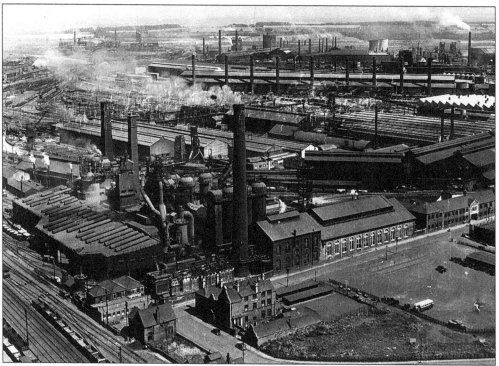

Frodingham Iron Works prior to closure in the early 1950s. The nine chimneys of Appleby Melting Shop, Redbourn Works and Appleby (North) Iron Works can be seen in the distance.

Frodingham Steel Works, shortly after it was built in 1890. Behind it is the old chemical works which burned down early in the 1900s.

The Four Queens of Scunthorpe in 1954. They are Queens Mary, Bess, Anne and Victoria Blast-Furnaces and ore beds. These are world record breakers and the pride of the town.

North Lincoln Iron Works, built in 1866. It closed in 1930 and is now the site of Appleby Coke Ovens.

North Lincoln Iron Works looking south from the rail yards.

This very pictorial photograph of a saddle tank loco at Redbourn Blast-Furnaces is one for the steam enthusiasts. Redbourn Iron Works started production in 1872 as the Redbourn Hill Iron & Coal Company. It was named after the area on which it was built, known by the locals as Red Burn Hills and not as most people think, after the village of Redbourne.

Redbourn Iron and Steel Works prior to its closure and the blowing up of its blast-furnaces in 1980. This photograph was taken before the closure of Appleby Melting Shop in 1983 and eight of its nine chimneys can be seen on the top right. The Queens Blast-Furnaces are on the top left.

Clugston Slag Works, *c.* 1962, with Redbourn's Blast-Furnaces upper right and Appleby Coke Oven gasometers in the upper middle of the photograph.

Blowing up Lindsey Ironworks in 1905. These works started production in November 1873 as the Lincolnshire Iron & Smelting Company Ltd. It was purchased by Redbourn in 1883 and re-named Lindsey Works.

The local people who came to see the blowing up of Lindsey Iron Works.

Appleby Iron Works. This was the sixth Iron Works to be built, in 1876. It later became the North Iron Works of Appleby-Frodingham. It was known to many as the 'Frozen North'. The neat hills created by the 'Sanders' removing the overburden in Trent Mines can be seen.

Appleby Steel Works, *c.* 1950. Showing the Melting Shop, Plate Mills, Canteen, Metallurgy Department and the Welfare Offices.

Normanby Park Works, *c.* 1915. The Normanby Park Works of John Lysaghts was the only integrated Iron and Steel Works to be built in Scunthorpe. It came into production in 1912. This is one of the author's favourite pictures of the works, with the bus in the foreground, on its way to Burton.

Normanby Park Works from the air, in full production after the building of the LD/AC Oxygen Steel Plant.

The last charge at the LD Plant, 25 February 1981.

The last pint at the Normanby Park Works Wet Canteen, 13 March 1981.

Two

Crosby and Frodingham Road

Frodingham Road showing the Centenary Methodist Chapel. It opened in 1908 and was burnt down in 1970.

Building the Crosby Hotel, 1910.

The men who built the Crosby Hotel were employees of Thornhill Brothers, builders from Lincoln. The architects were Mortimer & Son.

The newly-built Crosby Hotel, Normanby Road.

The bowling greens and rose garden at the rear of the Crosby Hotel. The man on the right is the gardener. The two girls are the daughters of Mr Beck, the licensee.

Old Crosby at the turn of the century, looking east towards Normanby Road.

Crosby Road, Ferry Road and Frodingham Road junction, looking down Ferry Road.

An early view of Diana Street.

Members of Diana Street Chapel in the early 1900s.

The old Tin Tabernacle, affectionately called the 'Tin-Tab' was used by St George's parishioners prior to the church being built, and was consecrated on 3 October 1925. This shows it decorated for a harvest festival. It was used as a church hall when the church was opened.

Crosby Elementary School, built in 1908.

Crosby School, after the erection of the memorial to the Crosby men who died in the First World War. Layne's shop, on the corner, is shown in the next photograph. Note the open-topped bus.

Layne's shop, Frodingham Road, in the 1920s.

Some of the builders of Holy Souls Roman Catholic Church, 1911.

The Consecration Ceremony of Holy Souls Church, 1911.

Frodingham Road and Holy Souls Church shortly after the consecration.

The Centenary Methodist Chapel, Frodingham Road. Opened 21 October 1908 it was burnt down in 1970.

Burke Street, *c.* 1910.

Normanby Road showing the Social Club (the Big Social) and the Crosby Hotel.

Three

Scunthorpe, the High Street to the Trent

St John the Evangelist Church area shortly after 1919, showing the 'Dreadnought' tank at the east end.

Scunthorpe from the top of the Frodingham Blast-Furnaces before Brigg Road was built.

Scunthorpe's first Library and the Constitutional Club. The library was opened by Joseph Cliff on 17 February 1904. The Constitutional Club burnt down in the early 1930s.

A south east view from St John's Church Tower, c. 1966. The Blast-Furnaces of the North Iron Works, Redbourn and the Appleby-Frodingham 'Queens' can be seen on the skyline. The old Public Library, Eva Brothers scrapyard and the Court House/police station can be seen along with the old Lincolnshire Road car bus depot.

This view was taken shortly after the flats were built in 1966. In the foreground is the stable yard of the Furnace Arms and in the distance Normanby Park Works. The flats were built to house the families from the east end of town which was due for re-development. The first person to move into the flats was Mrs Doris Cooke and her brother and sister-in-law, Mr and Mrs C.W. Dixon, were the next.

Left: Billy Hilbert, carved on the north west window of St John's church. He lived in a little whitewashed cottage facing the church. Right: 'Granny Hogg', carved on the south side of Billy Hilbert. She had a little emporium near the church building site. Some believe that the carving is Billy Hilbert's sister, but the Hogg family still live in Scunthorpe and assure the authors that this is 'Granny Hogg'. She died in 1902.

St John the Evangelist Church, built in 1891 in the gothic style. The church square was the first shopping area in the parish of Scunthorpe. The clock mechanism was installed when the church was built but there was no money to buy the clock faces. These were fitted in 1893 when the cost was raised by public subscription. This scene is with the 'Dreadnought' tank at the east end. St Johns was de-consecrated in April 1984.

36

Demolishing the old cast iron horse trough in St John's Church Square in the 1950s. The Scunthorpe Road Safety Committee complained that it interfered with the flow of traffic. On the site there is now a small island to control the traffic. Note Lingard's cycle shop on the corner.

The corner of Church Square and High Street. The imposing building on the right is the Provincial Bank. This was taken over in 1937 by the Local Council to become the Municipal Offices.

The High Street, Home Street junction. The shop on the left is Fletcher's chemist, Cutts & Taylors, the outfitters, is on the corner of Home Street. This shop later became a grocery branch of the Co-op. In the distance is the Blue Bell Hotel.

The same view as the previous photograph but taken just before the re-development of the area in the 1960s.

The Blue Bell Hotel, the Empire Theatre and the new brick Market Hall. The Market Hall was opened on 2 March 1906 by Lord St Oswald. The Blue Bell Hotel was demolished in the 1960s re-development scheme and the Empire Theatre was built in 1895, originally as the Public Hall. It burned down 24 May 1942. Binns store is now on the site of the Empire Theatre.

A horse market in 1904. The building in the background is the abattoir. The open market came under the control of the Scunthorpe Council on 21 January 1904. Before this R.I. Swaby, licensee of the Blue Bell Hotel, had inaugurated a small sheep market.

Ketch's sweet stall in the Market Hall. They made their own sweets but also sold Reads sweets, who had a factory in Dunstall Street, and Radiance sweets, whose factory was in Gilliatt Street where the Liberal Club now stands.

The market frontage, looking west, *c.* 1966.

The market frontage, looking east, *c.* 1963.

The corner of High Street and Market Hill, *c.* 1966.

The open market, *c.* 1966.

The covered market, *c.* 1966.

The covered market, *c.* 1966.

An aerial photograph of the market and the Blue Bell area in the early 1920s. There is much of interest to be seen in this photograph, including three Wesleyan chapels, the old Red Lion and the fairground site which later became the bus station. One chapel was behind Greenwood's shop until the re-development, another became Kirman's ironmongers and the other became the Sydney Hall cinema. Both of these buildings are still standing at the top of Market Hill.

The old Scunthorpe village pump at the top of Market Hill. The man is un-loading crates of Tadcaster Ales at White's off-licence.

Bells grocery shop at the corner of Market Hill and High Street, *c.* 1900.

Melia's store on the corner of Market Hill and High Street, *c.* 1910. Notice the price of bacon; six pence halfpenny a pound and sliced, for less than 3p.

High Street looking towards Wells Street/Cole Street, *c.* 1920.

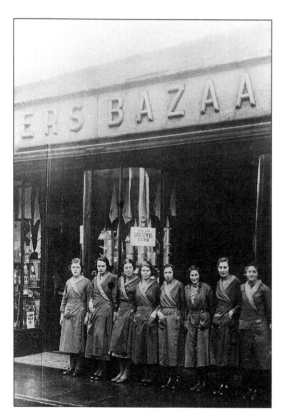

Pipers 'Penny Bazaar' and the staff in the 1920s. Note the wellington boots worn by some of the staff. Piper's Bazaar had wooden flooring and a pleasant smell of moth balls that everyone seems to remember.

High Street looking towards British Home Stores in the 1950s. Below Eleeses hairstylist was the Mazara Cafe, which no-one seems to remember, and also Tom Fisher's butchers shop.

High Street looking towards the Blue Bell Hotel in the 1950s. In the upstairs rooms of the building by the side of the Curry's van was the County Club.

High Street at the Wells Street/Cole Street junction. This photograph was taken before the fire at Bee's shop in 1912. The Midland Bank now stands on the opposite corner.

Cole Street looking towards Wells Street showing the stylish double arcading on the right and Halfords shop on the left.

Cole Street, Scunthorpe.

The Salvation Army Citadel and the Palace Theatre. The Scunthorpe Post Office was built in 1915 on the open space between the Palace Theatre and the arcaded buildings. The Salvation Army Citadel opened in 1907 and closed in 1996. The Palace Theatre became the Savoy Theatre in 1938, then the Essoldo Cinema, Classic Cinema, Pennywise store and finally the Poundstretcher store. It is now due for demolition.

The Higher Elementary School (Brown School) and the Liberal Club. The school was opened 30 August 1909 and demolished in 1995. The Liberal Club moved to its current site in Gilliatt Street on the site of the old Bethal Town Mission.

Wells Street in the 1920s.

Wells Street looking towards Cole Street, 1915. The Wesleyan Trinity Methodist chapel, now British Home Stores, is on the left. The nurses home is the building on the right. Miss Caddy was in charge of the nurses home in the late 1920s.

High Street just before the building of the London City and Midland Bank on the Wells Street corner.

A 1950s picture of Bee's shop with Woolworths on the right. Bee's shop was built in 1902 and Woolworth's first shop was opened in 1891.

Midland Bank, Woolworth's, Heslam House and Littlewoods in the 1950s. Heslam House was originally the Primitive Methodist chapel. It was bought by Mr Heslam for £5,000 who turned it into a furniture store. Fred Ayre was the first manager.

The Scunthorpe Primitive Methodist Chapel. The foundation stone was laid 15 July 1890. It closed in 1934 and became Heslam House with the local tax office renting the upstairs rooms.

An 1890s view of High Street and the Wesleyan Chapel.

The same view as the previous photograph but about fifty years later.

Scunthorpe High Street, c. 1910. The mangle on the left stands outside Robinson's ironmongers. The High Street was originally called Frodingham Road and Robinson's shop was No. 1. From Robinson's down to the church was called Town Street. The trees on the right are in the front gardens of Dr Reid and Dr Couldrey's houses. The spire of the Bethal Town Mission can just be seen above the houses. This was a tin building which later, the spire was removed, was 'jacked-up' on pine logs and with four horses and some of the children from Gurnell Street School, was dragged and pushed to a new position in Gilliatt Street. Note the fire hydrant on the right hand side, which was installed in 1906.

View of the High Street, looking east, c. 1925. The opticians spectacles are outside Maxwell's shop. There were two well-known opticians in the High Street and their slogans were: 'See Well, Maxwell' and 'See Moore, See Better'.

The High Street in the 1930s. On the left are Littlewoods, Heslam House and Woolworths. On the right, Alexander's tailors and Timpsons shoe shop.

This High Street view shows Holder Brothers music shop and Pott's Cosy Cafe on the left.

A 1950s eastwards view looking from Ravendale Street.

This 1890s photograph has Ravendale Street on the right and Gilliatt Street on the left. This view of St John's church is not yet obscured by buildings.

The Scunthorpe Fish Merchants and the Colonnade is shown on the left. The houses on the right have not yet been bought by business people and turned into shops.

The High Street looking east from Frances Street corner. The Oswald Hotel on the right is now the Tavern in the Town. Munro's on the opposite corner is now the Abbey National Building Society.

Looking west from Frances Street, *c.* 1915. This shows Moore's opticians and the dome of the Co-op building. Across the road is Sky, not the satellite television station but a high class gents outfitters. At the top of the street is a horse-drawn bus, the Blue Bell Flyer.

The same view as in the previous photograph but about twenty years later. Baguleys corner shop is now Tandys electronics shop.

The High Street West, *c*. 1930. The Jubilee Cinema re-opened on 2 June 1930 after 'cleaning, decorating and the installation of the new western electric sound system'. The notice on the Co-op building is advertising 'Superb Western Electric Talking Pictures' which dates the photograph.

Scunthorpe High Street looking east, *c*. 1950. This scene is very much as it is today except that the businesses have changed hands. The imposing Co-op Emporium building now houses Index. It was built in 1930.

A similar view as in the previous photograph but about thirty years earlier when High Street was called Frodingham Road and the houses had not yet been converted into shops.

The Britannia Hotel with the *Scunthorpe Telegraph* newspaper seller outside, *c.* 1950. This man was a familiar sight for years, selling papers in all weathers.

Oswald Road in the 1950s. The Congregational church on the right was dedicated 4 April 1912 after building at a cost of £3,040.

The Majestic Cinema and Oswald Road in the 1940s.

The Geisha Roller Skating Rink on Doncaster Road (originally called Clayfield Road). In 1912 it became the Pavilion Cinema but everyone continued to call it 'The Rink', although the younger people never knew why. The site is now mainly occupied by eating establishments.

The inside of the Geisha Roller Skating Pavilion. When it was converted into a cinema the name 'Pavilion' was retained.

Occupation Lane, which is now Doncaster Road. After the Keadby road/rail bridge was built in 1916, a new road was needed to link it directly to Scunthorpe, so Doncaster Road was built and Occupation Lane became a memory. The first lines of Edith Spilman Dudley's poem of Occupation Lane are clearly depicted in this picture, 'Deep ruts in a grassy old highway, 'Twixt hedges of briar and thorn'.

The new Doncaster Road. It was built by unemployed workers during the 1920s depression.

The first bridge over the River Trent. The rail link and bridge was completed in 1864, but the road traffic from Scunthorpe still had to go via Gainsborough to cross the river. One of the spans pivoted on the pier to allow two routes through for shipping.

The King George V Road/Rail Bridge. This bridge was completed in 1916 and operated on the same principle as Tower Bridge in London, using the weight of a water counter balance tank. The King opened the bridge but the plaque recording the event has since 'gone missing'.

Four

Frodingham

Brumby Wood Lane, Frodingham.

Brumby Wood Lane, *c.* 1920.

Jubilee Cottages, Brumby Wood Lane built as retirement homes for Appleby-Frodingham workmen. The land was purchased in 1918 and their back gardens gave the residents free access to the Brumby Hall sports grounds.

St Lawrences Church before it was enlarged in 1913. The church was built in 1236.

Water Lane, Frodingham. This is the junction of Oswald Road, Howden's Hill and what is now, Station Road. The photographer is standing in Church Lane. This area was knocked down in the 1920s to build Station Road.

Oswald Farm, Frodingham. The large building in the middle distance is the same one that can be seen at the bottom of Water Lane in the previous picture. The farm belonged to R.I. Swaby, the licensee of the Blue Bell Hotel. This postcard was sent to a Miss Fieldson in 1906.

Wortley House. This was built by the Cliff Brothers and named after Wortley near Leeds, where they had a plumbago works. A younger brother, Philip Cliff, resided at the house until 1884 so the house must have been built in the late 1870s or early 1880s. Maxmilian Mannaburg lived here when he came to Scunthorpe to commence steelmaking. It is now the Wortley House Hotel.

Frodingham National School, built by Rowland Winn in 1865. This was a very generous and far-sighted act by Rowland Winn before the days of an Education Act and when children were being used as cheap labour in the mines and factories. The school was enlarged in 1874 and is still in use today.

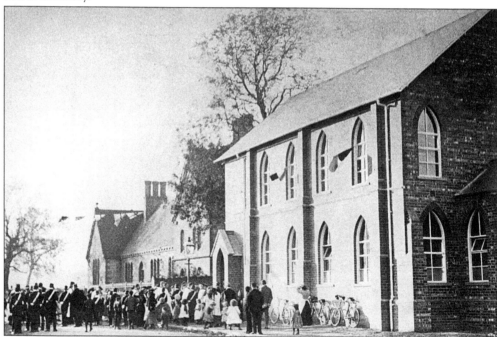

The opening of the Frodingham Institute, 21 October 1905. In the late 1940s the Institute was used by Gurnell Street School. The ground floor was used for girls cookery lessons and upstairs was used by the boys as an extra classroom, when the school leaving age was raised from 14 to 15 years in 1948.

The Frodingham Council Offices and the Wesleyan Chapel, on the corner of Cottage Beck Road and Trent Street. The chapel has long since gone but the council offices later became a maternity hospital and then the Scunthorpe Museum. The Scunthorpe Camera Club used rooms at the museum for many years.

Frodingham Feast, 1936. The man with the pipe is Mr Drain. His two daughters, Edie and Martha, are next to him and the lady between the two men is Mrs or Miss Holden.

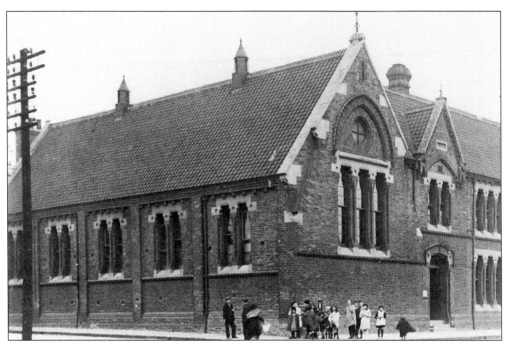

Frodingham Hospital. It was built by Rowland Winn in 1871 as a public hall, at a cost of £100. In 1886, eight beds were added and it became a Cottage Hospital. In 1937 it opened as the Coronation Club and is still flourishing.

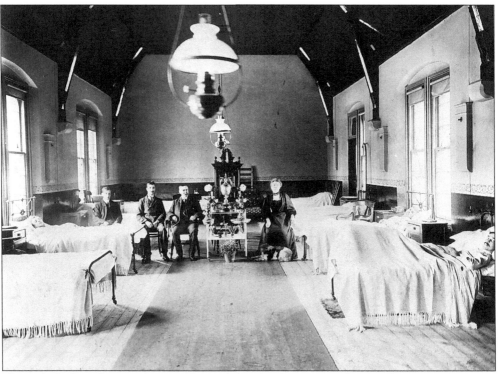

The eight beds in the new Cottage Hospital shortly after it opened in 1886.

Five

Brumby

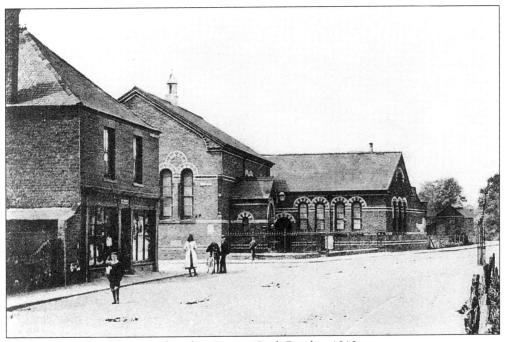

The New Brumby Wesleyan Chapel in Cottage Beck Road, *c.* 1910.

Cottage Beck Road, c. 1910. This road is the approximate boundary of Brumby and Frodingham (with Brumby on the south side).

Chapel Street, New Brumby. New Brumby was built by Earl Beauchamp and old Frodingham by Rowland Winn.

Brumby Hall in the late 1800s. The first reference to the building was made on 11 November 1390, when Robert and Johanna Wasslyn resided there. It is believed that there has been a settlement around the site from pre-Anglo-Saxon times. A spring rises in the area and used to flow away as a stream. The spring still flows in Brumby Hall basement and is pumped away. Brumby Hall eventually came into the control of the Appleby-Frodingham Estate Company and is today used as a nursing home.

The Methodist Chapel, Ashby Road, Old Brumby. This was knocked down when the new St Mark's chapel was built.

Thompson's Garage, Ashby Road. This is now the Shell garage adjacent St Mark's chapel.

The same building as seen in the previous photograph but photographed in the mid-1800s.

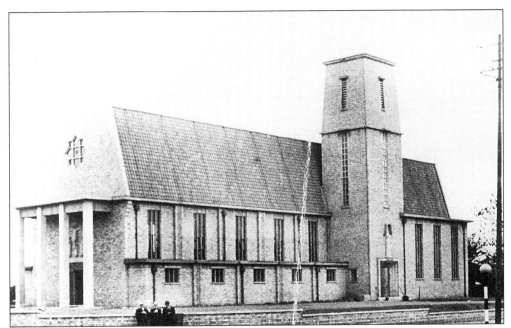

St Hugh's Church, Brumby Corner. Built in 1939. The swan weather vane of St Hugh has not yet been erected.

Old Brumby Street at the turn of the century.

Rose's or Rose Cottage, Old Brumby Street, *c*. 1920.

Mr and Mrs Skelton of Brumby. It was said, 'He selt best hossshit in village 'cos it 'ent n'straw in it'.

The Old Brumby village pump.

The Old Brumby Farmhouse, *c.* 1910. It still stands today.

The Brumby bridle path looking back towards Brumby. This path led through to Ashby and is now Revesby Avenue.

View of the bridle path looking south. The house on the right still stands.

Six

Ashby

Ashby Turn, looking east down Ashby High Street, *c.* 1950.

Mill Lane during road works, looking east. The name Mill comes from the Ashby Post Mill that stood just back from the Ashby Turn and was demolished in the 1890s. Mill Lane is now Ashby High Street.

Mill Lane looking towards Ashby Turn in the 1900s.

Ashby High Street at the Bottesford Road junction. The man in the white coat is thought to be 'Brassy' Sharman, a well known local character. Note the village pump.

The Crown Hotel and the Primitive Methodist Chapel. The chapel was built in 1885 and the last service was held in 1960. It was demolished in 1962 and is now the site of the Ashby Market. The white cottage is the Crown Hotel. The new Crown was built on the side of the existing building and on completion the remains of the old hotel were pulled down.

A similar view to the previous photograph showing the new Crown Hotel. Note the little boy in the distance shovelling up manure for his dad's roses!

A view of the old Crown looking west.

Ashby High Street and the old post office. The white cottage on the right is the post office. The Ashby war memorial now stands on the site.

The Primitive Methodist Chapel, looking west, *c.* 1900. The sign on the eaves reads 'Jackson, Draper and Outfitter'.

The first St Paul's Church. This Tin Tabernacle was bought by the vicar, with his own money, and opened in 1899. It was replaced by the new St Paul's in 1925 and stayed as a church hall for a short time.

An old view of Ashby High Street looking east. The street is illuminated with oil lamps and the oil cart can be seen on the right.

The Screeds, looking north, *c.* 1910. The correct name for the Screeds was Kirton Terrace. The washing is believed to be the football kit of Ashby Institute Football Club.

A charming old photograph of Column Lane.

The first Wesleyan Chapel in Ashby High Street. The school house was set back alongside it. In 1907, when the current chapel was built, Ashby Institute moved in. The building was demolished in July 1972.

The new Wesleyan Chapel built in 1907. The white cottage was knocked down to build Stockshill Road. The village stocks were reputed to have stood near this site.

The High Street and old Brown Cow Hotel, *c.* 1907. The new Brown Cow was built at the back of the old one which was knocked down to become the car park.

The new Brown Cow Hotel.

The east end of Ashby High Street, looking west, c. 1910. The new Wesleyan chapel can be seen in the distance. The pony and trap possibly belonged to Dales the butchers.

Lower Ashby High Street, c. 1950. Byron Turner's chemist shop is on the left and the Co-op store is on the right. This photograph was found stuck on the wall of a derelict house with electrician's black tape. It took a little work to clean it up!

Seven

The Charter
Celebrations

The Coat of Arms for the new Borough of Scunthorpe. The blast-furnace on the helm represents the industry, the fossil shells, the ironstone and the chain represents the five villages linked as one, and the sheaf the agricultural past. The motto 'The heavens reflect our labour' refers to the red glow in the sky from the molten metal and slag casting.

Left: The rejected Coat of Arms. The flames from the furnace were not thought to be aesthetically pleasing. Right: The Civic Seal for the new Borough.

The Royal Seal appended to the Charter.

The official ceremony for the 'Handing Over' of the Charter, 10 October 1936. This photograph shows the police leading the procession up the High Street.

The Charter Mayor, Sir Berkeley Sheffield, and the Civic Party proceeding to the Old Show Ground. He is accompanied by Lady Sheffield and the Deputy Charter Mayor, A.E. Dowse. The mace was a gift from the Co-op Mutual Plate Glass Company.

The Princess Street families and the street decorations.

More decorations in what is believed to be Sutton's Row.

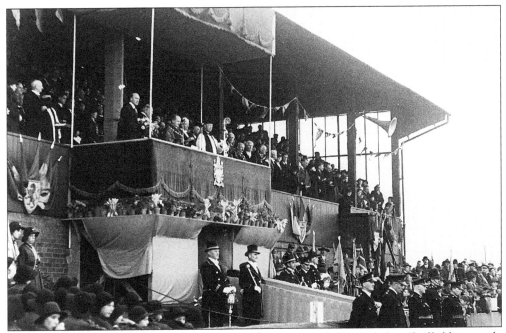

The stand and presentation platform at the old showground. Sir Berkeley Sheffield was only mayor for the day, then the mayoral duties were taken over by his deputy. He generously donated the mayoral chain of office. The mayoress's chain was presented by the Lincolnshire Ironmasters Association and the deputy mayor's chain by the Scunthorpe and District Building Trades' Employers' Association.

Sir Berkeley Sheffield. He is seen receiving the charter from the Right Honourable Earl of Derby KG, PC, GCB, GCVO. In the wig is the genial face of the charter town clerk, James Frederick Auld, and by his side is the Bishop of Lincoln.

The civic party visiting one of the local works, probably Normanby Park.

The Earl of Derby being greeted, by the town clerk. It is interesting to note that the Charter of Incorporation begins: 'Edward the Eighth, by the grace of God of Great Britain, Ireland and the British dominions beyond the seas, King, defender of the faith, Emperor of India.' So, the charter was granted by the King who was never crowned but the seal on the charter is that of King George the Fifth.

Eight

Transport

A local-built bus ready for delivery.

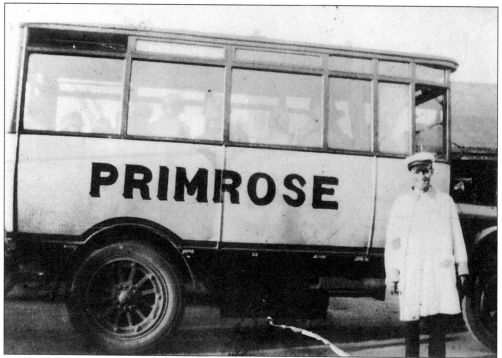

A 1920 Garford bus from the Primrose Bus Company. This has a 1924 body, four cylinders, travelled at 25 mph and was the first bus with pneumatic tyres. The Primrose Bus Company was owned by the Hornsby family.

F. Hornsby, owner and driver of this 1921 Dearborn, outside the Dolphin Hotel, Cleethorpes.

Enterprise and Silver Dawn Bus Station in Scunthorpe High Street, opposite Market Hill.

The High Street Bus Station just before its closure and relocation in the 1960s.

The first railway station in town, sited just north of the Frodingham Blast-Furnaces. These are the crowds that awaited the return of Rowland Winn after he won a court battle with Earl Beauchamp in 1867 over the ownership of part of Brumby East Common. The gentleman in the stovepipe hat is the station master. The wall is adjacent to Frodingham Iron Works.

The second railway station was built in 1887 about 200 yards west from the first.

The third and current Scunthorpe and Frodingham Railway Station built in 1928.

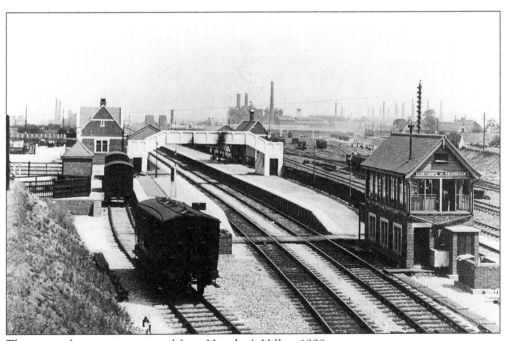

The new railway station, viewed from Howden's Hill, *c.* 1928.

The Normanby Park Steel Works chauffeur and car, *c.* 1912.

The Lincolnshire steam roller outside Munro's Drapers in Scunthorpe High Street. The Abbey National Building Society is now on the site of Munro's.

Nine

People, Places and Events

Garden Party at Brumby Hall, c. 1946. Back row: A.C. Dobson (Church Warden), Revd Muxlow (Curate), Canon Rust, Mr Turrell, (Laypreacher). Front row: Revd John Swaby (Vicar), Mrs Walshaw of Brumby Hall, the Bishop of Lincoln and Mrs Muxlow.

The Zeppelin over Frodingham Blast-Furnace, 31 January 1916.

On the night of 31 January 1916, Scunthorpe was attacked by a Zeppelin airship. It stayed only eight and a half minutes but during that time it dropped twenty high explosive bombs and more than fifty incendiary bombs. It was miraculous that only three people were killed and so little damage done. The first bomb landed in Ravendale Street at 10.45 pm blowing the backs off four houses. This was followed by a large number of bombs dropped on Glebe Pit. It then flew over Trent Cottages in Dawes Lane, dropping an incendiary bomb through 86 year old Mrs Markham's roof just as she was getting ready for bed. She calmly threw a bucket of water over it, and with the help of a neighbour, tossed it out of the window. The Zeppelin travelled over North Lincoln Iron Works Yards and Redbourn Works, up North Lincoln Road to the Chemical Works Corner, over Frodingham Iron Works and North Lindsey Works Yards. At Redbourn it killed Tom Danson of Park Street, Jack Cyril Wright of Ashby High Street and Wilkinson Benson of Ethel Terrace was killed in Lindsey Yards. Many people suffered from shock and concussion and a good deal of superficial damage was done.

Left: A hand-held bomb dropped by the Zeppelin Right: The fire at Bee's Shop in 1912.

Crowds watching the fire at Bee's Shop. Note the photographer with his camera and tripod on the wall of the Wesleyan chapel. He could be taking the picture above.

The Old Steamer, Scunthorpe's first fire engine. It was presented to the town in 1907 by Sir Berkeley Sheffield. Fire-chief Sudlow, a local lay preacher and councillor, is on the left. Fire hydrants had been installed in 1906. This fire engine was the latest design of its type and was most likely used at Bee's shop fire.

The Fire Brigade in 1953 with Station Officer Waterlow, Sub-Officer Asquith, L.F.M. Caton and firemen: Glover, Gleadhill, Brown and Act. and Divisional Officer Reynolds.

The Scunthorpe Police at the Old Show Ground being inspected at what is thought to be the Home Office Review. The uniformed figure on the left is Superintendent 'Long Joe' Hutchinson who came to take charge of the local police force in 1927. 'Long Joe' was well known in Scunthorpe as the man who once raided seven pubs in one hour! He retired in March 1932, a much loved and respected figure.

The Scunthorpe Police Special Constables in 1945, with Superintendent R.F. 'Reg' Knowler, another respected police-chief.

The Lincolnshire Motor Cycling Club, Scunthorpe Centre Hill Climb, *c.* 1910.

Five intrepid Scunthorpe cyclists at the Hull Velodrome. The date is not known but the photograph was probably taken in the 1910s. The occasion is thought to be when the cyclists broke the world cycle speed record. On their first trial run, they had not allowed for banking and shot off the edge off the track.

Albert 'Lal' White. Lal was a leading figure in the local, national and international cycling fraternity. In 1924 he won a silver medal at the Olympics and held fifteen national titles.

Mr Woolsey with his hackney and carriage. The hackney won its class at the Brussels Exhibition shortly before the First World War. Mr Woolsey had a saddlers and leather goods shop in Scunthorpe High Street.

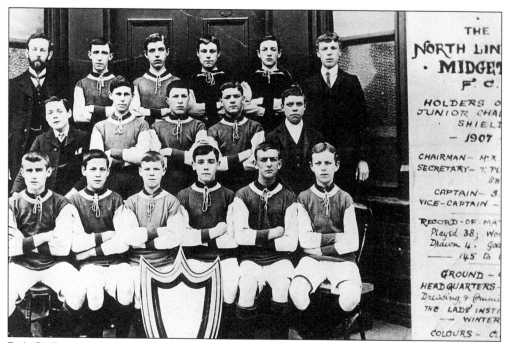

The text visible on the right side of the photograph reads:

THE
NORTH LIN[...]
· MIDGET[...]
F. C.

HOLDERS O[...]
JUNIOR CHA[...]
· SHIEL[...]
— 1907

CHAIRMAN — M[...]
SECRETARY — T. T[...]
8[...]
CAPTAIN — 3[...]
VICE-CAPTAIN —

RECORD · OF · MA[...]
Played 38; Wo[...]
Drawn 4. Go[...]
145 to [...]

GROUND — [...]
HEADQUARTERS —
Dressing & Annu[...]
THE LADS' INST[...]
— WINTER
COLOURS — Cl[...]

R.A.C. 'Reggie' Symes and his North Lindsey Midgets Football Team. Reggie was a local solicitor who formed St John's Church Bible class, later to become 'The Keenites'. The football team was formed from his Bible class boys. In 1910 they merged with Scunthorpe Town Football Club to become Scunthorpe United. Their playing field was near the Oswald Hotel until they bought the old Show Ground in 1919.

The wedding of Mrs Archer to Mr Gelder. The photograph was taken outside 'Glenryst', Cemetery Road near Bushfield Road junction, the home of D.J.K. 'Dave' Quibell's father and stepmother. Dave Quibell was later to become Lord Quibell and Quibell Park sports ground was named after him.

Mr Podmore's butcher's shop in High Street, which was later purchased by Dick Long. Situated in the block between the bus station and Cole Street. It shows Tom Pinder the errand boy, Tom Fisher, Dick Long, ? Podmore and Herbert Clayton, another errand boy. Tom Fisher opened his own butchery business and Herbert Clayton started a drapery business.

Fletchers Butchers also in the lower High Street area in the 1920s.

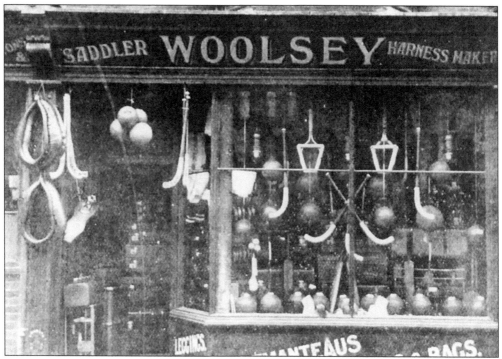

Woolsey Saddler and Harness Maker, *c.* 1920. His shop was at the lower end of the High Street almost opposite Home Street.

Callister's Model Bakery, 147 High Street in 1912. The man in charge of the horse is Mr Callister. The cart is loaded with 1,500 pounds of bread and 800 rolls for the Normanby Show. The little girl, who can just be seen looking out of the upstairs window is thought to be Miss Montieth.

The British Legion Band, outside the Cricket Pavillion at Brumby Hall Sports Ground, *c.* 1930. Back row: ? Banks, Tom Bogg, -?-, -?-, -?-, Teddy Burke, Jack Thurston, -?-, -?-. Middle row: Tom Hunt, -?-, -?-, -?-, Bob Cawood, Len Cooke, -?-, ? Couch. Front row: ? Banks, ? Gray, Tommy Cloe, Jack Gilboy (Bandmaster), Mr Harrison (President), 'Long Joe' Hutchinson (Drum Major), ? Cloe, ? Barr, -?-, -?-. The two boys sitting are Tommy Banks and Eddie Burke.

The Ashby Subscription Band, 17 July 1935. They are outside the Globe Cinema in Ashby High Street after the presentation of their instruments. Mr Kendall, the conductor, worked at Appleby-Frodingham Works. After the Ashby Band was disbanded he started the Appleby-Frodingham Works Band utilising, it is thought, the musical instruments and some of the old members of the Ashby Band.

The school children of the first Wesleyan Chapel in Scunthorpe, c. 1870. This chapel was situated at the rear of Greenwoods shop and was demolished, along with Greenwoods, during the re-development of that area in the 1960s.

Children from the Arthur Howden's School at Frodingham. The more wealthy parents paid for their children to go to this private school (obvious by the quality of their clothing). The teacher at the back is Miss Howden, Arthur's daughter, who took the school over from her father. The General Post Office on the corner of Church Lane is its approximate site.

The Scunthorpe Business and Professional Men's Forum, on their visit to the Humber Bridge building site, 1977. The man pointing is the site engineer, John Hyatt, who became a member of the Forum during the construction period. Some of those featured are: Fred Ayre, Brian Motson, Peter Howlett, Bert Clifford, Eddie Leonard, Reg Cooke, Ted Andrew, Tom Cribb, John Robinson, Steve Poole, Phillip Rowley, John Teall, Syd Lingard, Gerald Godson, Albert Smith, Rex Benham and George Bowskill.

Her Majesty the Queen and Prince Phillip in the Royal Procession as it travels down the High Street, 1954.

This line-up, photographed in about 1935, are: Roy Thomas, Ted Cheesman, Cliff Drury, Ken Ferriby, Don Roberts and Clem Harsley, a band that played weekly at dances held in the Victoria Rooms at the Furnace Arms, during the 1930s. Ted and Don were hairdressers, Clem worked at Appleby-Frodingham Iron Works and Roy was a builder.

Lance Mallalieu MP, electioneering at the Chemical Works corner bus stop, Brigg Road, in the 1950s.

Mrs Mallalieu receiving a bouquet from Diana Martin at a garden party, *c.* 1950. The party was held in the grounds of the old St John's vicarage, now 'The Hollies' rest home. The group comprises A.C. Dobson, (newsagent and tobacconist), Mrs Mallalieu, Revd John Swaby (vicar), Lance Mallalieu MP, and 'Taffy' Williams, (a Gurnell Street school teacher). Messrs Dobson and Williams were the church wardens.

Contract erectors labour dispute 1952-53. This took place during the building of the Seraphim project at Appleby-Frodingham. The dispute followed a demand for increased 'height money'

and pay increase up to 3/4d (17p) an hour. They are seen here marching up Scunthorpe High Street.

Jack Rook in fancy dress, outside Dobsons Tobacconists, ready for the annual Hospital Carnival, c. 1930. The suit is covered with silk flags which were gifts in BDV cigarette packets and were sewn on by his wife. Jack worked for the Night Soil Department in Winterton Road as a night watchman when the 'dilly carts' were emptied. He also cleaned the public lavatories on weekdays. He was a well-known character walking from toilet to toilet with a hosepipe and brush over his shoulder, wearing rubber waders and with a huge Irish Wolfhound at his side.

Uriah Long's flour mill, near the old police station, *c.* 1900. It was built around 1888 and went out of use shortly after this picture was taken. It is now the Old Mill restaurant and bar.

A Civic Procession in 1902. They are celebrating the Coronation of Edward VII and Alexandra and are just passing Gilliatt Street in the High Street.

The Cobbler's Boy at either Picks in Home Street or Broomheads opposite the Furnace Arms.

A Brief Chronicle of Scunthorpe

1236	St Lawrence church, Frodingham was built.
1809	The first Wesleyan chapel built, situated behind what is now Greenwoods shop.
1838	Gates erected at the roads into Scunthorpe village to keep out stray livestock.
1858	About the time that Uriah Long's flour mill was built.
1859	The re-discovery of ironstone.
1860	The first ore was mined. The first ironstone 'Chuckers' were paid one farthing a ton. The start of the railway to link the Trent, Ancholme & Grimsby Line with the South Yorkshire Line and spanning the Trent with a railway bridge. It was completed in 1864.
1861	A second Wesleyan chapel was built to seat 300 on the east side of what is now Market Hill. The old one became a Sunday school (it seated only 40 people).
1862	The building of Trent Ironworks started by the Dawes Brothers.
1863	The building of Frodingham Ironworks started by Joseph Cliff.
1864	Trent Ironwork's furnace was 'blown-in'. First cast 26 March.
	R.I. Swaby succeeded Johnnie Huteson as the landlord of the Blue Bell Hotel.
1865	Frodingham Ironwork's first furnace was 'blown-in'. First cast in May. Wrecked by an explosion in August.
1866	North Lincoln Ironwork's built. Its first furnace was also wrecked by an explosion.
1867	Rowland Winn financed the building of Frodingham School and school house.
1870	Underground mining boreholes started about this time.
	The 1870s was a period of acute depression.
	The first Primitive Methodist church built on Crosby Road.
	The New Brumby Primitive chapel built on Cottage Beck Road.
1871	Rowland Winn built Frodingham Town Hall at a cost of £100.
1872	Redbourn Hill Iron and Coal Company built two furnaces.
	Scunthorpes first post office built on, what is now, Market Hill.
1873	The Lincolnshire Iron & Smelting Company started operation.
1874	29 April, a group met in Enoch Markham's home at No.1 Chapel Street to form the Scunthorpe Co-operative Society. The first shop opened in his front room.
1875	Pig Iron Carriers were paid two pence ha'penny (1p) per ton of iron carried.
	The Frodingham vicarage was pulled down and a new one built. It is now the museum.
1876	Appleby Ironworks 'blew-in' their first furnace.
1877	The Lincolnshire Congregational Union held their first meeting to establish a Congregational Communion.
1878	Struggles started for Unions to be recognised by the Ironmasters.
	The Milton Hall, in Manley Street, was built for the Congregationalists.
1880	A mission was formed for the Scunthorpe parish. It met in a Tin Tabernacle, (Tin Tab) at the top of Dawes Lane.
1884	The Scunthorpe Mission moved from the Tin Tab to the Assembly Rooms in Manley Street.
1885	Rowland Winn built a school for girls and infants on the old Station Road.
	The Primitive Methodist chapel in Ashby High Street was built, which is now the market site.
1885/86	The Brass and Iron foundry, called 'Nibblem Clink' by the locals, opened adjacent the Trent Ironworks.
1886	Frodingham Town Hall was fitted with eight beds to become Frodingham Cottage Hospital.
1887	The second railway station was opened (adjacent to Frodingham Ironwork).
	Crude steel was produced at Frodingham but the process was not viable.
1888	16 August, the Salvation Army was established in the Temperance Hall, Home Street. The Station Hotel was built opposite Frodingham Ironworks.
	In September, the Co-op Central Store on Winterton Road was opened.
1889	Maxmilian Mannaburg came to Frodingham Ironworks to build and run a steelmaking plant.
	The Primitive chapel in Crosby Road was gutted by fire.
1890	First steel 'tapped' at the re-named Frodingham Iron & Steel Company.
	In March, the Ecclesiastical parish of Scunthorpe was formed.
	15 July, the foundation stone for the new Primitive Methodist chapel was laid in the High

Street. It was opened in 1891. Woolworths in Scunthorpe High Street now occupies the site.

22 December, the first meeting of the new Scunthorpe Urban Council was held.

1891 Wednesday 15 April, the new Scunthorpe parish church of St John the Evangelist, was consecrated by the Bishop King of Lincoln.

1892 In January, the Lincolnshire Ironmasters Association formed.

St Johns church vicarage was built on Normanby Road.

2 November, a Roman Catholic service was held. The first in Scunthorpe for hundreds of years.

1893 Rowland Winn, 1st Baron St Oswald, died at his home, Nostell Priory, Wakefield.

The clock faces were fitted to St Johns church.

1894 A very harsh winter which gave blast-furnace men many problems.

Brumby and Frodingham joined together and were given urban status.

1895 The Gurnell Street Church of England School was built.

The Scunthorpe Court House was built.

The Scunthorpe Public Hall was built on the corner of Town Street (High Street) and Cods Lane (Manley Street).

1896 The Scunthorpe Co-op Society was 21 years old.

On 10 October, the Ashby Co-op Branch opened (No. 2 branch).

1899 Scunthorpe obtained gas rights to the town.

A Tin Tabernacle extension was added to Frodingham Cottage Hospital.

1900 The Frodingham works replaced gas lighting with electricity.

5 June, the fourth Wesleyan chapel opened on the corner of High Street and Wells Street. It is now the site of British Home Stores

1901 6 May, Scunthorpe's first gas works opened, which is now the site of Baths Hall.

1902 'Granny Hogg' died. Her face is carved on St Johns church along with Billy Hilbert's.

1903 Scunthorpe's rates were three shillings and four pence (17p) in the pound and Frodingham's only ten pence (4p).

10 August, Joseph Cliff laid the foundation stone for Scunthorpe's first library in old Station Road.

1904 17 February, the new library was opened by Joseph Cliff.

1905 The first mechanically charged blast-furnace in Europe was commissioned at Frodingham.

The North Lindsey Light Railway opened which ran from Frodingham to Whitton, approximately 10 miles.

1906 2 March, the second Lord St Oswald opened the new Market Hall.

6 March, the cattle market was inaugurated.

Easter Monday, the Ashby Free Library opened.

1907 The Scunthorpe Citadel of the Salvation Army opened. It closed in 1996.

Sir Berkley Sheffield gave Scunthorpe its first fire engine, which was named *The Old Steamer*.

1908 28 January, formation of the Scunthorpe Co-op Womens Guild.

21 October, the new Centenary Methodist church on Frodingham Road opened.

The Crosby Elementary School was built.

1909 15 April, blast-furnace men went on strike over a reduction in wages, which lasted five weeks.

30 August, the Higher Education School (Brown School) opened in Cole Street.

31 August, the Scunthorpe Museum was opened in the Station Road Library.

In August, the Scunthorpe Fire Station opened.

1910 10 October, the new, large, Co-op store in the High Street was opened.

The Scunthorpe Town Football Club merged with North Lindsey Midgets to form Scunthorpe United Football Club.

1911 Construction started for John Lysaghts Normanby Park Works.

The Holy Souls Roman Catholic church opened on Frodingham Road.

1912 Crosby applied for urban status but was rejected.

The Geisha Roller Skating Rink became the Pavillion Cinema.

4 April, the Congregational church at Britannia Corner was opened.

Normanby Park Works first furnace was 'blown-in'.

A national coal strike bankrupted the Appleby Iron Company and the lease was taken over by the Frodingham Iron & Steel Company in June and they restarted ironmaking.

1913 Scunthorpe, Crosby and Ashby amalgamated as an Urban District.

13 January, Clayfield Road (Doncaster Road) Elementary School opened.

The St George's Iron church was opened in Frodingham Road.

1914   Charles Chatburn, a foreman at Frodingham Ironworks, left the works, bought a bus and called it *Enterprise*. This was the birth of the Enterprise & Silver Dawn Bus Company.

The Co-op started using a motor lorry for furniture removal instead of horse and cart.

1915   The pre-crushing of ironstone began.

In May, the amalgamation of Scunthorpe and Frodingham postponed until after the war.

The new post office in Cole Street opened.

1916   16 January, Zeppelin attack on Scunthorpe and the Ironworks.

A new road/rail bridge was built over the River Trent, along with a new line and viaduct.

1917   Frodingham Iron & Steel Company joined the United Steel Company in partnership with Appleby Iron Company but they retained separate boards.

1918   The Appleby and Frodingham Works Athletic Club formed.

The outbreak of the war nullified an appeal for funds to build a church at Crosby.

The Scunthorpe Co-op became affiliated to the Brigg Divisional Labour Party.

Mr D.J.K Quibell was elected first parliamentary candidate for the Brigg Division.

1919   In March, Scunthorpe and Frodingham were administratively united.

Start of the post war depression years.

Scunthorpe United bought the Old Showground from the Parkinson Trustees.

The Brumby Hall playing fields were laid out. The iron gates were made by the Clarke Brother's Blacksmiths at South Ferriby, from metal supplied by Frodingham Ironworks.

1920   In June, Guest, Keen & Nettleford bought Normanby Park Works from the Berry Group and added a fifth blast-furnace.

The Baptist church was formed. It met in the home of Mr and Mrs Blomfield in Shelford Street.

Scunthorpe post office upgraded to head office status. Mr H.C. Coman was postmaster.

1921   From 1921 to 1923 there was a severe recession and most works closed down at some period. During works shut downs, the workers gave their time to levelling and preparing Brumby Hall sports grounds and erecting the fencing facing Ashby Road.

1922   In October, the Baptist church opened in Scunthorpe.

The Co-op announced the building of a new model bakery in Clay Lane (Rowland Road). It was burnt down on Sunday 19 March 1995.

1923   LNER absorbed the other railway companies operating locally.

16 November, new gas works at the top of Dawes Lane commenced producing gas.

Normanby Park Works Working Men's Club was formed on works premises. 'Complying with club laws and approved by friendly societies, to supply alcoholic refreshment, in moderation, to employees during working hours'.

1925   The old gas works on Doncaster Road closed.

A new engine driven *Merryweather* fire engine was bought to replace the *Old Steamer*.

The Scunthorpe Co-op's 50th Jubilee Year.

The Model Bakery opened on 19 January.

On Saturday 25 July, the North Lindsey Light Railway closed. It was later used by ore trains.

3 October, St George's church, Crosby was consecrated.

15 October, Crosby became a parish.

Parliamentary approval was given for LNER to improve the railway and sidings locally.

In February, Redbourn Hill Iron & Coal Company Ltd was wound up and the assets transferred to Richard Thomas & Company Ltd.

It was about this time that Normanby Park Coal Club started.

1926   14 November, a war memorial was unveiled on Doncaster Road west of the Baths Hall.

W.T. Underwood Ltd took over both the Progressive and Drury's Enterprise & Silver Dawn Bus Companies.

1927   The Enterprise & Silver Dawn and the Progressive Bus Company were re-acquired by Drury.

In March, the App-Frod Coal Club started.

Sunday 17 July, a new railway bridge opened on Howden's Hill, Ashby Road.

17 September, Woolworths opened their first store in High Street.

15 October, Lady Astor opened the Scunthorpe Grammar School.

1928   Sunday 11 March, the current railway station opened.

Thursday 28 June, the opening of the new 400 feet road bridge over the railway at Brigg Road.

30 July, the current re-inforced concrete footbridge to Frodingham opened.

1929	8 December, Scunthorpe War Memorial Hospital opened in Cliff Gardens.
1930	North Lincoln Ironworks closed.
	The Co-op Emporium was built in Scunthorpe High Street.
1931	Frodingham Iron Company purchased the North Lincoln Ironworks.
	The parish pump in front of Woolworths, and the Brumby and Ashby pumps were removed.
1932	The Municipal Swimming & Slipper Baths were opened.
	The LNER loco sheds, south of Dawes Lane, were opened.
1933	26 October, the Duke of Kent, then Prince George, opened the New War Memorial Hospital, the nurses home and the new Scunthorpe trunk road (Kingsway and Queensway). He also visited the Normanby Park and Appleby-Frodingham Works.
	The Appleby and Frodingham works amalgamated to become the Appleby-Frodingham Works (App-Frod), of the United Steels Company.
	The Royal Hotel was built.
1934	24 February, the Primitive Methodist chapel in High Street closed. It became Heslam House Furniture Store, with the tax office upstairs.
1935	Trent Ironworks were scrapped.
1936	10 October, Scunthorpe Charter Celebrations took place.
	Joseph ('Pop') Campbell opened his School of Ballroom Dancing.
	In May, the Maternity Home opened in Brumby Wood Lane (demolished 1995).
1937	The Frodingham Hospital opened as the Coronation Club.
1938	The building of the South Iron Works commenced. It added two new blast-furnaces, blowing engine house, sinter plant and coke ovens at App-Frod. The new coke ovens were built on the site of the North Lincoln Ironworks.
	The introduction of the 48 hour working week.
1939	The National Grid was connected to Scunthorpe. Until this time the local works supplied their own electricity, and the town used Ap-Frods surplus power.
	Brumby Hall Sports Club was erected.
	30 March, South Iron Works commenced full production.
	All the works received their 'black-out' instructions.
	The Scunthorpe Youth Centre opened.
	Thursday 2 March, the new head post office on the corner of Howdens Hill opened.
1940	01.05am 28 June, the South Iron Works were bombed.
	1 August, King George VI and Queen Elizabeth made an unannounced visit to Scunthorpe and visited the Normanby Park and App-Frod Works.
	Women become a major force in the steel industry as more men were 'called up' for the war.
1942	24 May, at 2 am, the Empire Theatre burnt down. It was originally the Public Hall. At the time of the fire it was a force's canteen.
1944	Redbourn's parent company merged with Baldwins Ltd and became Richard Thomas & Baldwins Ltd.
1945	July, there was a general election. The nationalisation of the Iron and Steel Industry was part of the Labour Party's manifesto.
1946	The App-Frod Works Band formed under the baton of Mr Kendall.
	A shortage of labour in the industry. Voluntary workers from Europe, mainly displaced persons, were recruited.
1947	The first steel was produced in the new Frodingham Melting Shop at South Iron Works.
1948	The whole of Normanby Park's Steel Plant was re-modelled.
1949	The bill to nationalise steel was finally made law but was delayed by the 1950 general election.
1950	The Enterprise Bus Company nationalised.
	The start of the closure of Frodingham and Appleby Works prior to the coming on stream of the two new blast-furnaces and sinter plants at South Iron Works in 1952.

Bibliography

100 Years of Ironmaking at Appleby-Frodingham H.S. (Ben) Ayres
Technical Survey of the Iron and Steel Works of Appleby-Frodingham, Iron and Coal Trades Review
Technical Survey of Richard, Thomas & Baldwins Iron and Coal Group Trades Review
Appleby-Frodingham News, Various Editions
Appleby-Frodingham Chronicle, Various Editions
A Short History of Redbourn Works, P.F. Bell
Jubilee History, Scunthorpe Co-operative Society
Lysaghts, Scunthorpe, G.K.N. Group
Lysaghts, Scunthorpe Works, Steel Times, 5 March, 1965
History of Scunthorpe and Frodingham, H. Dudley
History of Appleby-Frodingham, Walshaw & Berhendt
'Men of Iron, Men of Steel'. *100 Years of Steelmaking in Scunthorpe*, Reg Cooke
'Ironmen', Jack Owen
The History of British Steel, John Vaizey
South Ironworks, App-Frod Steel Company
Village Days, Scunthorpe Museum Publication
An Industrial Island, Scunthorpe Museum Publication
The Great Central in LNER Days (2), David Jackson and Owen Russell

Acknowledgements

Our sincere and grateful thanks are extended to the many people of the town who have allowed us to copy their precious photographs. To our son Peter, for keeping an eye on our narrative, for helping with the layout and for acting as arbitrator. A special thank you to John and Valerie Holland for allowing us free access to their collection and for their continued support. To British Steel, Sections, Plates & Commercial Steels at the Scunthorpe Works. To Gordon Davison, David Davies and Chris Mimmack of the Video Section and Photographic Department for free access to the Works archives and to 'The Picture Company' in Ashby. Finally, our gratitude and respect for those early photographers who fortunately recorded our past including, A.H. Singleton, T. Hemstock, J. Spavin, F. Brown, G. Hall, J. Westoby, Francis Bowen.

Reg and Kathleen Cooke